WEDDINGS
for Choirs

40 perfect SATB pieces

Compiled and edited by
Judy Martin and Peter Parshall

MUSIC DEPARTMENT

OXFORD
UNIVERSITY PRESS

OXFORD
UNIVERSITY PRESS

Great Clarendon Street, Oxford OX2 6DP, England
198 Madison Avenue, New York, NY10016, USA

Oxford University Press is a department of the University of Oxford.
It furthers the University's aim of excellence in research, scholarship,
and education by publishing worldwide

Oxford is a registered trade mark of Oxford University Press
in the UK and in certain other countries

1 3 5 7 9 10 8 6 4 2

ISBN 0-19-353265-4

Music and text origination by
Barnes Music Engraving Ltd., East Sussex
Printed in Great Britain on acid-free paper by
Biddles Ltd., Guildford and King's Lynn.

PREFACE

Music almost always features in the wedding ceremony, serving both to enhance and reflect the unique nature of the occasion. This collection is primarily intended to act as an abundant resource for the wedding choir, offering both the familiar 'classics' and extending the repertoire with many unearthed 'gems' and newly-commissioned delights by the likes of Malcolm Archer, Bob Chilcott, and Gabriel Jackson. Additionally, in much the same way that the bride and groom will have had access to a wealth of knowledge and advice when choosing their venue, celebrant, and caterers, this anthology may provide the couple with similarly rich, diverse, and informed choices when selecting their choral music.

Each contribution to the collection is suitable for general use during the wedding and, furthermore, many of the pieces are also particularly suitable for specific parts of the ceremony. We have tried to include a wide selection of settings of texts commonly associated with weddings, many in versatile new arrangements, including J. S. Bach's 'Jesu, joy of Man's desiring', Schubert's 'Ave Maria', Mozart's 'Laudate Dominum', and Wagner's 'Here comes the bride'. Among the specially commissioned pieces, Philip Moore's 'How do I love thee?' and Ian Crew's 'Now lies the earth' are invaluable settings of secular texts, whose inclusion in this compilation illustrates, and caters for, the increasingly varied nature of the wedding ceremony.

Pieces are presented alphabetically by title, and suggestions for usage of particular settings are indicated in an index provided below the list of contents.

We are very grateful to all those who have contributed to *Weddings for Choirs* and, not least, to the choir of St Mary's Wallingford and to the RSCM Southern Cathedral Singers, who have acted on our behalf as willing choral 'guinea pigs' for some of the selections we have made.

JUDY MARTIN
PETER PARSHALL
August 2002

INDEX OF TITLES AND FIRST LINES

Where the first lines differ from titles, the former are shown in italics.

*For anthems in foreign languages with English translations,
the titles in both languages are shown in Roman.*

Pieces suitable for unaccompanied singing are marked thus *.

INDEX OF COMPOSERS AND ARRANGERS

Where the first lines differ from titles, the former are shown in italics.

*For anthems in foreign languages with English translations,
the titles in both languages are shown in Roman.*

*Pieces suitable for unaccompanied singing are marked thus * .*

SUGGESTED WEDDING USAGE

Where the first line differs from the title, the former is shown in italic.

For anthems in foreign languages with English translations, the titles in both languages are shown in Roman.

Pieces suitable for unaccompanied singing are marked thus *.

LITURGICAL INDEX OF WEDDING CONTENTS

Where the first lines differ from titles, the former are shown in italics.

*For anthems in foreign languages with English translations,
the titles in both languages are shown in Roman.*

Pieces suitable for unaccompanied singing are marked thus *.

TITLE	COMPOSER / ARRANGER	NO.	PAGE
Advent			
Ave Maria	Charles Gounod and J. S. Bach, arr. David Blackwell	*3*	6
Ave Maria	Franz Schubert, arr. G. L. Martin	*4*	12
Hail O Mary	Franz Schubert, arr. G. L. Martin	*4*	12
*Rejoice in the Lord alway	Anon., ed. Peter Le Huray and David Willcocks	*34*	198
Maundy Thursday			
*A new commandment	Peter Parshall	*1*	1
Easter			
*Arise, my love	Joel Martinson	*2*	3
Come, my way, my truth, my life	John Clements	*7*	34
Hallelujah	G. F. Handel, ed. Clifford Bartlett	*14*	69
*Rise up, my love, my fair one	Healey Willan	*35*	206
Pentecost			
*If ye love me	Bob Chilcott	*20*	100
Annunciation and other Feasts of the BVM			
Ave Maria	Charles Gounod and J. S. Bach, arr. David Blackwell	*3*	6
Ave Maria	Franz Schubert, arr. G. L. Martin	*4*	12
Hail O Mary	Franz Schubert, arr. G. L. Martin	*4*	12
*I beheld her, beautiful as a dove	Healey Willan	*17*	94
*Rise up, my love, my fair one	Healey Willan	*35*	206
Funerals and Remembrance			
*Brother James's Air	James Leith MacBeth Bain, arr. Gordon Jacob	*6*	28
*Geistliches Lied	Johannes Brahms, ed. John Rutter	*9*	44
God be in my head	Andrew Carter	*12*	63
*God be in my head	John Rutter	*13*	67
*Lass dich nur nichts nicht dauren	Johannes Brahms, ed. John Rutter	*9*	44
*Let no sad thought oppress thee	Johannes Brahms, ed. John Rutter	*9*	44
*I will lift up mine eyes	Philip Ledger	*19*	98
*Set me as a seal upon thine heart	William Walton	*36*	208
*The Lord's my shepherd	James Leith MacBeth Bain, arr. Gordon Jacob	*6*	28

to Pom and Nadia on the occasion of their marriage.

1. A new commandment

John 13: 34–35

Peter Parshall
(b. 1971)

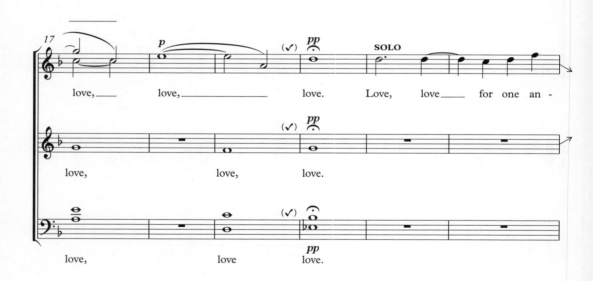

for Samuel Baker

2. Arise, my love

Song of Songs 2: 10–12; 8: 6–7*

Joel Martinson
(b. 1960)

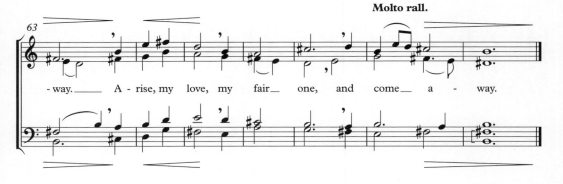

3. Ave Maria

The Angelic Salutation
English text by Neil Jenkins

Charles Gounod (1818–1893)
and J. S. Bach (1685–1750)
arr. David Blackwell

* This piece can also be performed by solo or tutti soprano and piano or organ, omitting the alto, tenor, and bass parts.

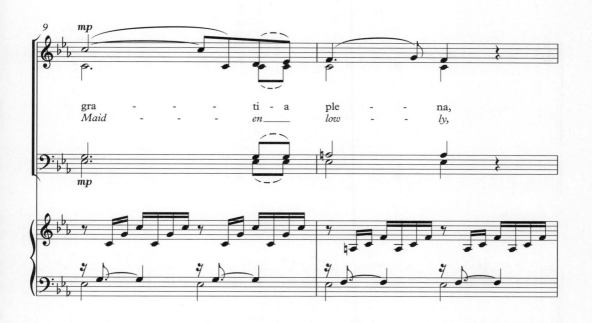

gra - - - - ti - a ple - - na,
Maid - - - *en___ low - - ly,*

Do - - mi-nus te - cum, be - ne -
Vir - - *gin___ ho - ly, bles - sed___*

4. Ave Maria

(Hail O Mary)

The Angelic Salutation

Franz Schubert
(1797–1828)
arr. G. L. Martin

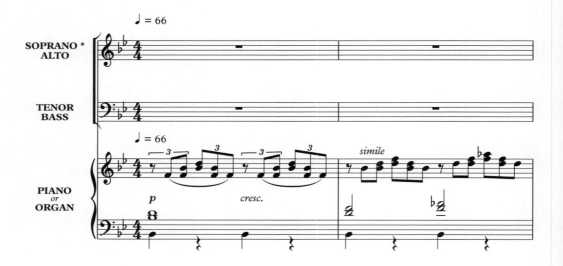

* This piece can also be performed by solo or tutti soprano and piano or organ, omitting the alto, tenor, and bass parts.

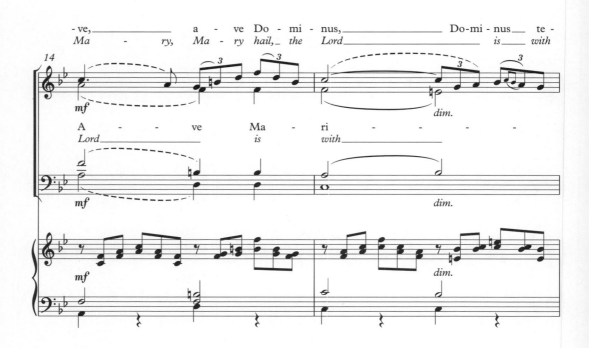

to Alan Gray and the Choir of Trinity College, Cambridge

5. Beati quorum via

Psalm 119: 1

C. V. Stanford
(1852–1924)

Translation: Blessed are those who are undefiled in the way, and walk in the law of the Lord.

Inscribed to William Hendry

6. Brother James's Air

(*The Lord's my Shepherd*)

based on Psalm 23

James Leith MacBeth Bain
(1860–1925)
arr. Gordon Jacob
1895–1984

by._____ He lead-eth me, He__ lead-eth me, The qui - et wa - ters

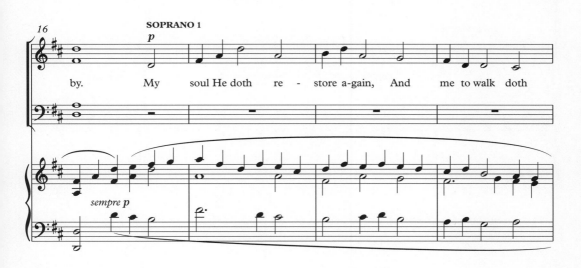

SOPRANO 1

by. My soul He doth re - store a-gain, And me to walk doth

sempre **p**

make With - in the Paths of Bless-ed-ness, E'en for His own Name's

(Organ sustain pedal D. Piano strike it again)

7. Come, my way, my truth, my life

George Herbert
(1593–1633)

John Clements
(1910–86)

* keyboard reduction for rehearsal only.

This piece (E144) is available separately (ISBN 0–19–351129–0).

for Mel Olson and the Zephyr Point Church Music Festival, Nevada, 1990

8. Deep Peace

v. 1: An old Gaelic blessing
vv. 2 and 3: Andrew Carter

Andrew Carter
(b. 1939)

Deep peace of the run-ning wave to you, Deep peace of the flow-ing air to you,

Deep peace of the qui-et earth to you,

This piece (A424) is available separately (ISBN 0–19–350479–0).

9. Geistliches Lied

(*Sacred song*)

Paul Flemming
(1609–40)

Johannes Brahms (1833–97)
Op. 30
ed. John Rutter

* Or piano, 3 or 4 hands [Brahms gives this as an alternative, but the pedal part should be played an octave lower if using only three hands.]

10. Gloria in excelsis Deo

(from *Gloria*)

Antonio Vivaldi
(1678–1741)
ed. Paul Everett

This movement is adapted from the vocal score of the OUP edition of *Gloria* (ISBN 0–19–338454–X).
Orchestral material is available for hire.

in memory of Grace Frankell

11. Go before us, O Lord

Adapted from the Book of Common Prayer

Andrew Carter
(b. 1939)

Words in italics are the original Book of Common Prayer text.

This piece (E167) is available separately (ISBN 0–19–351154–1).

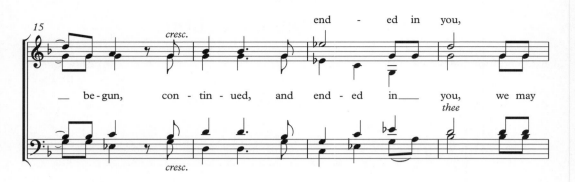

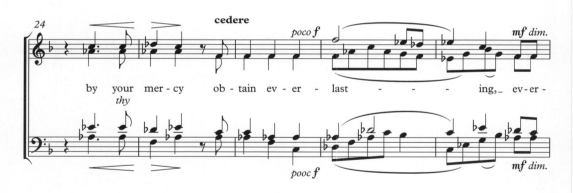

for Julian and Mandy

12. God be in my head

Book of Hours, Sarum, 1514

Andrew Carter
(b. 1939)

This piece (E159) is available separately (ISBN 0–19–351145–2).

13. God be in my head

Book of Hours, Sarum, 1514

John Rutter
(b. 1945)

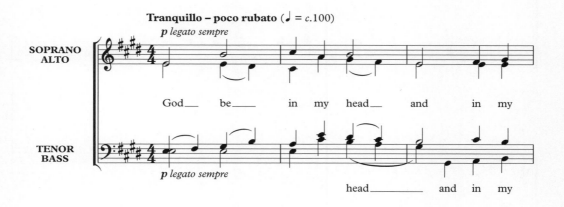

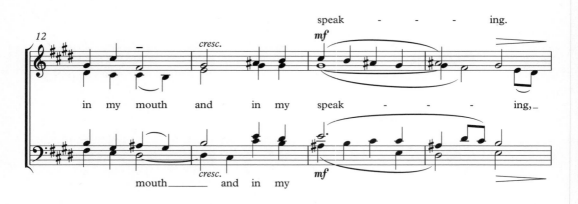

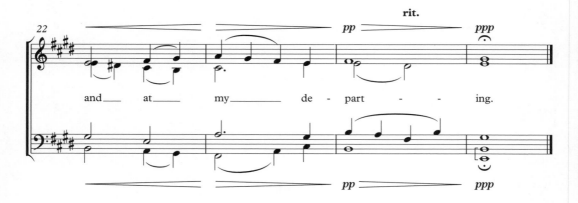

14. Hallelujah

(from *Messiah*)

Revelation 19: 6; 11: 15; 19: 16

G. F. Handel
(1685–1759)
ed. Clifford Bartlett

This movement is taken from the vocal score of the OUP edition of *Messiah* (ISBN 0–19–336668–1). Full scores and all orchestral material are available for sale or hire.

23

God Om - ni - po - tent reign - eth, Hal-le -

Hal-le - lu-jah, Hal-le - lu - jah, Hal-le-lu - jah,

-lu - jah, Hal-le - lu-jah, Hal-le - lu - jah, Hal-le-lu - jah,

Hal-le - lu - jah,

25

-lu - jah, Hal-le - lu - jah, Hal-le-lu - jah, Hal-le - lu - jah, Hal -

Hal-le - lu - jah, Hal - le - lu - jah, Hal-le - lu-jah, Hal-le -

for the Lord God Om - ni - po - tent

for the Lord God Om - ni - po - tent

Lords,   and He shall reign,   and

Lords,   and He shall   reign,_____   and He shall

Lords,   and He shall reign, and He_____   shall   reign,

Lords, and He   shall   reign for   ev – er and ev   –   er,

He   shall   reign   for   ev – er and ev –   er,   for ev-er and

reign_____   for ev – er and ev –   er,   King of Kings, for ev-er and

and He shall reign   for ev – er and ev –   er,   King of   Kings,_____

and He shall reign for__ ev – er and   ev – er, King of Kings, for ev-er and

[tr]

82

Kings,   and Lord of Lords,   King of Kings,   and Lord of

Kings,   and Lord of___ Lords,   King of Kings,   and Lord of___

Kings,   and Lord of___ Lords,   King of Kings,   and Lord of___

Kings,   and Lord of Lords,   King of Kings,   and Lord of

85

Lords,   and He shall reign for ev - er and ev -

Lords,   and He shall reign for ev - er and ev -

Lords,   and He shall reign for ev - er and ev -

Lords,   and He shall reign for ev - er, for ev - er and ev -

[tr]

15. Here comes the bride!

(an adaptation of 'Bridal Chorus' from *Lohengrin*)

Robin Barry

Richard Wagner (1813–83)
arr. The Editors
organ part arr. Malcolm Archer and others

A full version of this piece using Wagner's original words with the addition of a singing translation by John Rutter, can be found in *Opera Choruses* (ISBN 0–19–343693–0).

Christ be our guide when we de-clare: 'What God has bon-ded, let no man des-troy!' This ho-ly un-ion: hus-band and wife, Strength in com-mun-ion, rich-ness in life! Once, did our Lord in

old Ga-li-lee,___ joy-ful-ly bless this pro-found mys-te-ry.___

Blessed then are you in Christ's al-might-y name, for rich-er, for

poor-er, in joy or in___ pain.___ Praise God a-bove!

16. How do I love thee?

Elizabeth Barrett Browning
(1806–61)

Philip Moore
(b. 1943)

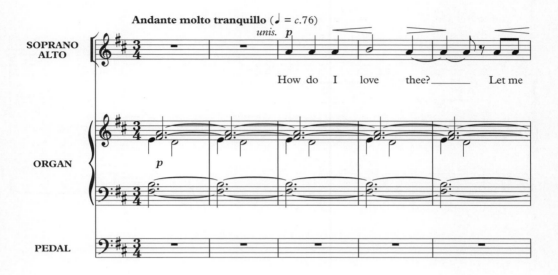

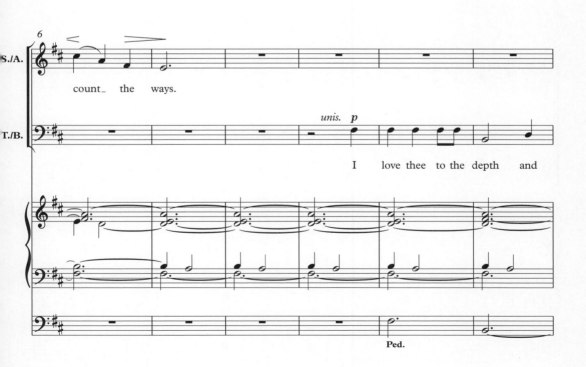

when feel - ing out of breadth and height__ my soul can reach,

sight__ for the ends__ of Be - ing and i - de - al Grace.

I love thee to the le - vel of eve - ry day's

un poco più mosso

most qui - et need,_

by sun_ and can - dle light._

un poco più mosso

I love thee free-ly as men__ strive__ for Right.

I love thee pure-ly as they turn__ from Praise.

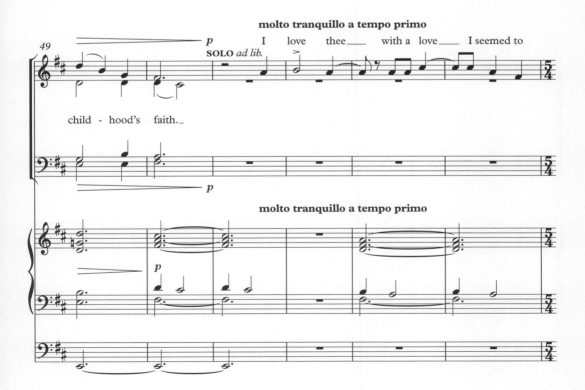

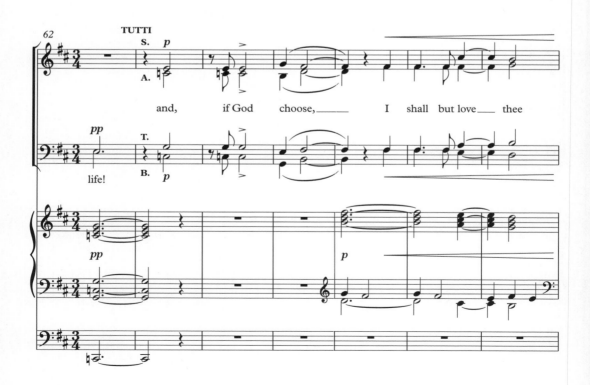

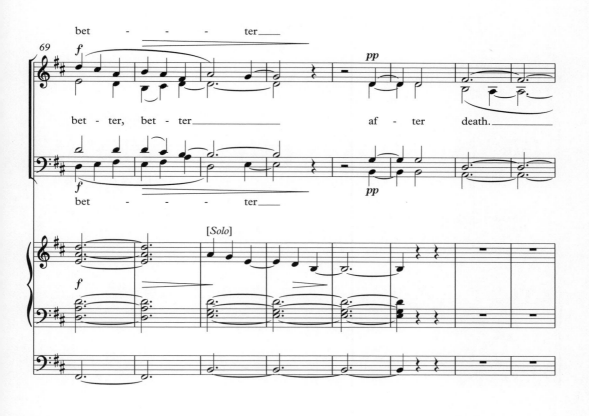

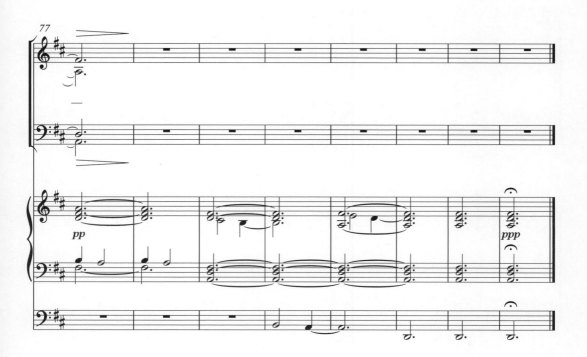

17. I beheld her, beautiful as a dove

From Responsories from
an Office of Our Lady (Eighth century)

Healey Willan
(1880–1968)

18. I sat down under His shadow

Song of Songs 2: 3, 4

Edward C. Bairstow
(1874–1946)

This piece (A4) is available separately (ISBN 0–19–350104–X).

brought   me,   He brought me____   to the   ban-quet-ing house,   and His
ban-quet-ing house,   to   the

brought   me   to   the

ban - ner   o - ver me,_ His ban - ner   o - ver me_ was   love,____

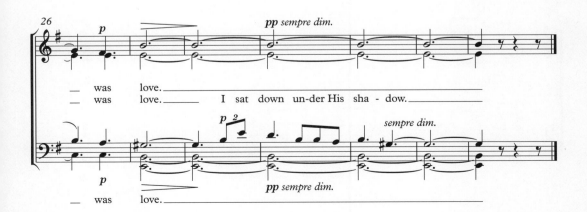

__ was   love.____
__ was   love.____   I sat down un-der His sha - dow.____

__ was   love.____

for John Tiarks, fifth Bishop of Chelmsford, on the occasion of his Enthronement

19. I will lift up mine eyes

from Psalm 121

Philip Ledger
(b. 1937)

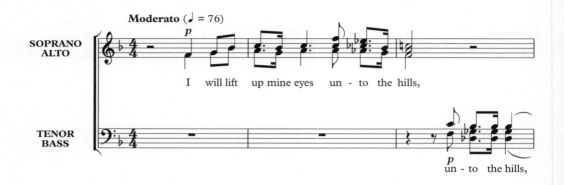

is thy keep-er,⸺ the Lord is thy de-fence⸺ up-on thy right hand;⸺

thy keep-er,⸺ thy de-fence,

ff marcato   molto dim. e rall.

⸺ So that the sun shall not burn thee by day,⸺ nei-ther the moon⸺

thy right hand; ff marcato

The Lord

⸺ by night.⸺ The Lord shall pre-serve thy go-ing out, and thy com-

The Lord

pp

- ing in, for ev - er - more.⸺

from this time forth⸺⸺ ev - er-more.

for Mark Toews and the Lawrence Park Community Church Choir, Toronto

20. If ye love me

John 14: 15–17

Bob Chilcott
(b. 1955)

for Grupo Vocal Olisipo

21. Irish Blessing

Traditional

Bob Chilcott
(b. 1955)

This piece (BC18) is available separately (ISBN 0–19–343229–3).

22. Jesu, joy of man's desiring

from Cantata 147

Martin Jahn
(*c.*1620–*c.*1682)
tr. Robert Bridges
(1844–1930)

Johann Sebastian Bach
(1685–1750)
organ part arr.
Malcolm Archer & Peter Parshall

* The middle stave has been arranged so that the manual parts can be played on a single manual instrument. For a simplified version or for performance with a piano, or organ with no pedals, leave out the middle stave.

Drawn by
Where the

thee,__ our souls__ as - pir - ing,
flock__ in thee__ con - fid - ing,

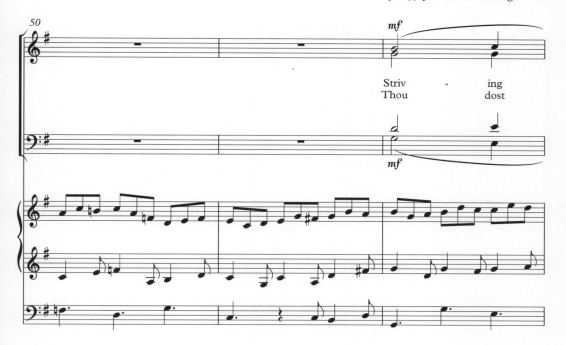

soar - ing,   dy - ing
in_____ the   love_____ of

round___ thy_____ throne.
joys___ un - known.

23. Laudate Dominum

(*O praise the Lord*)

from the *Solemn Vespers*

Psalm 117
English version
adapted by Neil Jenkins

W. A. Mozart
(1756–91)
arr. Judy Martin

This piece can be performed by soprano soloist and accompaniment, by soprano soloist and SATB choir and accompaniment, or by SATB choir and accompaniment alone.

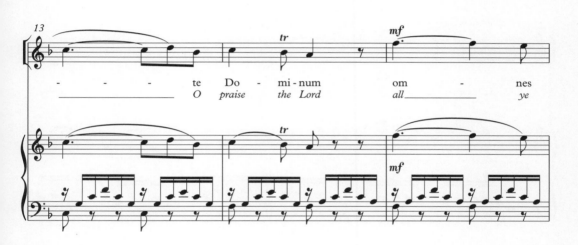

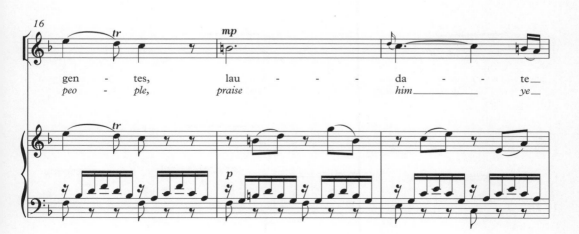

e - um   om - - - nes,   om -
na - tions,   *praise*   *him*   *all*

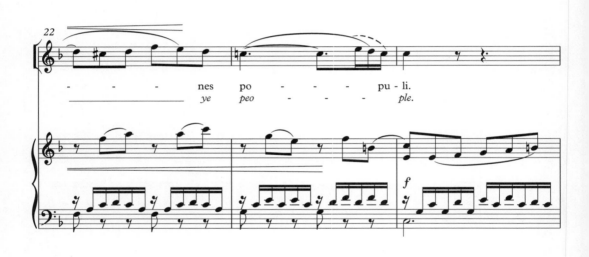

- - - nes po - - pu - li.
ye peo - - ple.

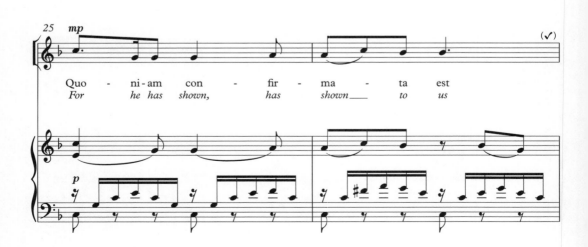

Quo - ni - am con - fir - ma - ta est
For   he has   shown,   has   shown___   to   us

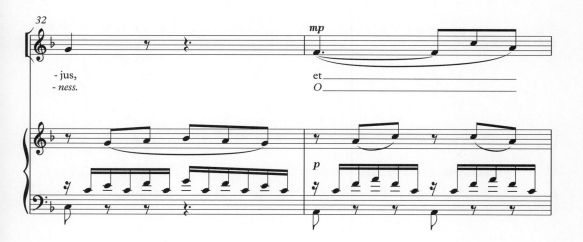

* If the piece is being performed by soprano soloist alone, the soloist continues to sing the top line of the choir parts.

† To omit the Gloria, cut now to the middle of bar 69, page 126.

by gracious permission the music to this anthem, composed by William Mathias, is dedicated to Their Royal Highnesses The Prince and Princess of Wales on the occasion of their Marriage at St Paul's Cathedral on Wednesday 29th July 1981

24. Let the people praise thee, O God

Psalm 67

William Mathias
(1934–92)

Steady, joyful, and majestic (♩. = c.72–6)

Let the peo-ple praise thee, O God: yea, let all the peo - ple

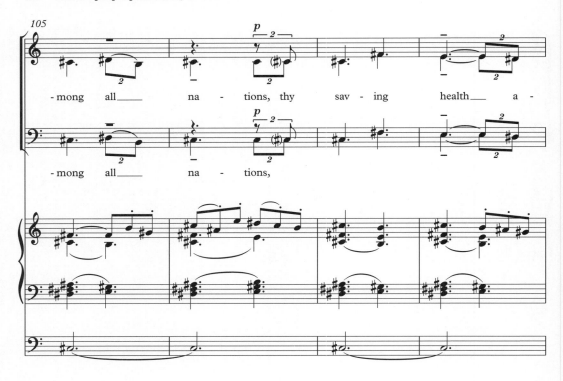

-mong all____ na - tions, thy sav - ing health____ a -

-mong all____ na - tions,

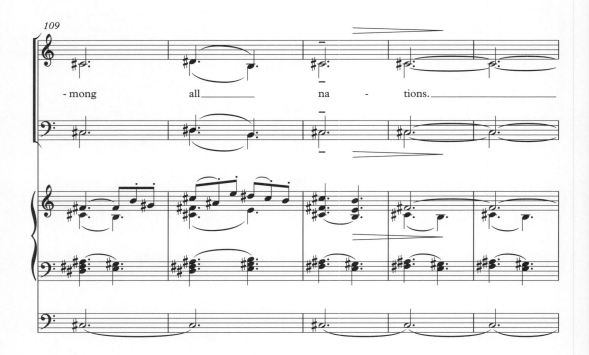

-mong all____ na - tions.____

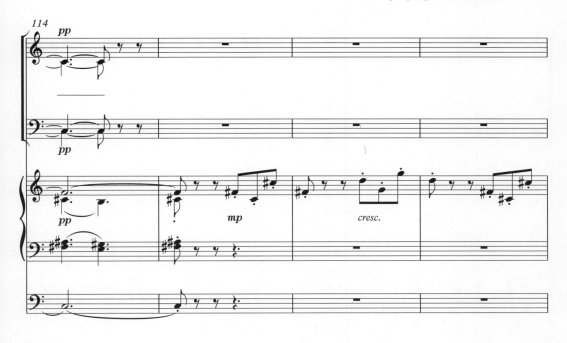

(Ped. D♭ optional)

25. Love

Alfred, Lord Tennyson
(1809–92)

Bob Chilcott
(b. 1955)

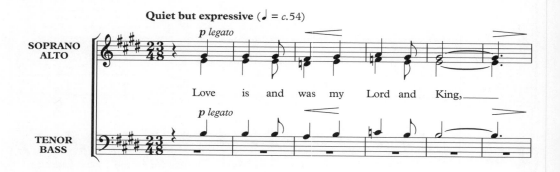

The original version of this piece (BC10) is a semitone lower. It is available separately (ISBN 0–19–343207–2).

* or a few soprano voices and solo tenor

† 'Lo-', sung as in 'Love'

26. My lovely one

(*Marriage Anthem*)

Edward Taylor (1646?–1729)
from *Sacramental Meditations*

Gerald Finzi
(1901–56)

* keyboard reduction for rehearsal only.

27. My true love hath my heart

Sir Philip Sidney
(1554–86)

John Rutter
(b. 1945)

This piece is no. 4 of *Birthday madrigals*, a five-movement choral suite written in 1995 for Brian Kay and the Cheltenham Bach Choir in celebration of the 75th birthday of the great jazz pianist George Shearing.

The complete *Birthday madrigals*, for mixed choir and double bass and optional piano, is published as a set (ISBN 0–19–338029–3). No. 1 (*It was a lover and his lass*), no. 2 (*Draw on, sweet night*), and no. 5 (*When daisies pied*) are also available separately. Upper-voice arrangements of nos. 1, 4, and 5 are also published.

This piece (X410) is available separately (0–19–343216–1).

28. Now lies the earth

Alfred, Lord Tennyson
(1809–92)

Ian Crew
(b. 1969)

Now sleeps the crimson petal, now the white;
Nor waves the cypress in the palace walk;
Nor winks the gold fin in the porphyry font:
The fire-fly wakens: waken thou with me.

Now droops the milk-white peacock like a ghost,
And like a ghost she glimmers on to me . . .

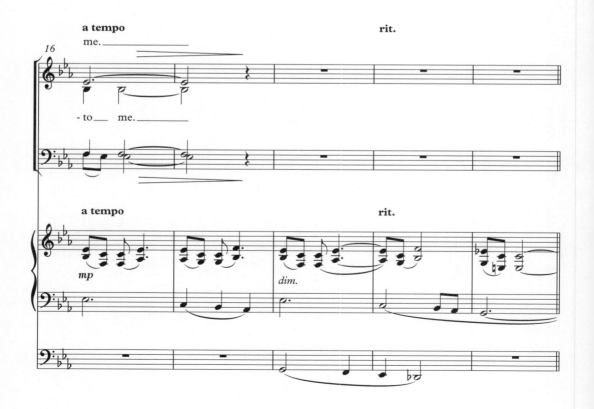

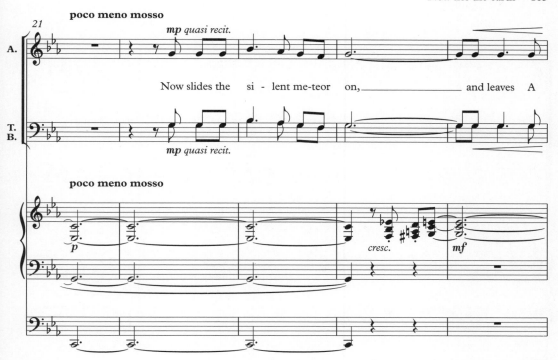

Now slides the si - lent me-teor on, _____ and leaves A

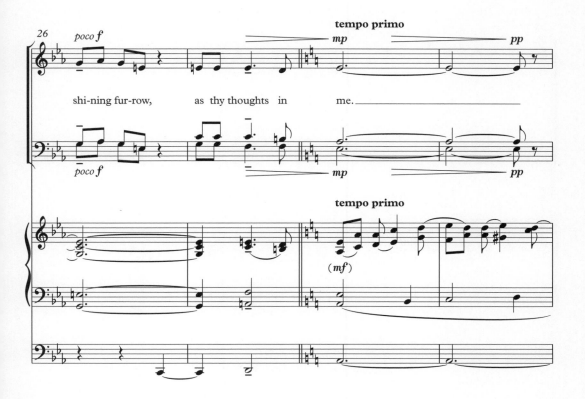

shi-ning fur-row, as thy thoughts in me. _____

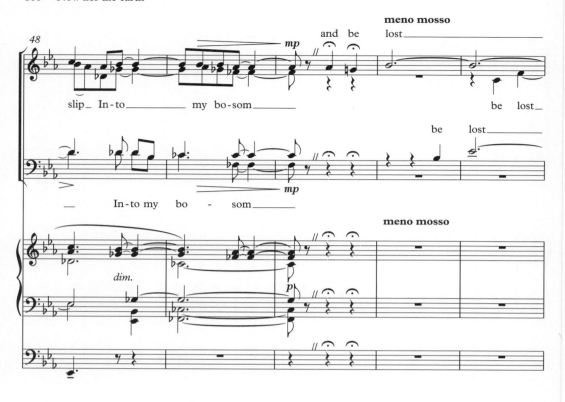

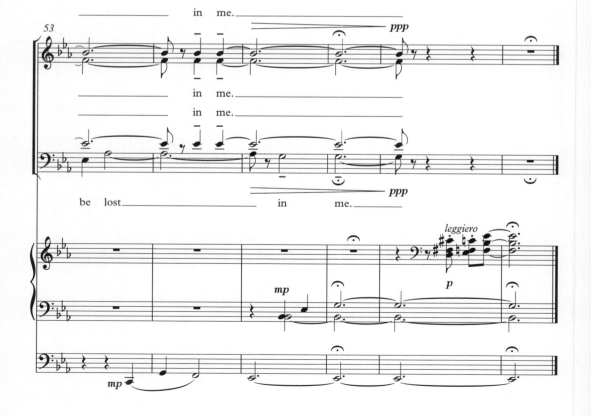

29. Now thank we all our God

(from *Cantata 79*)

Cantata 79
English Translation by
Catherine Winkworth
(1829–78)

J. S. Bach
(1685–1750)
arr. Peter Parshall

𝅗𝅥 = 76

ORGAN

f

S.
A.

ff

Now

T.
B.

f

thank   we   all   our   God,
won - drous   things   hath   done,

And

still   is   ours   to - day.

30. O sing joyfully

Psalm 81: 1–4

Adrian Batten
(1591–1637)
ed. Judy Martin

All dynamics are editorial.

16

f   *mf*

lute. Blow_____ up,   blow   up   the trum-pet   in the new moon: ev'n

f   *mf*

lute. Blow   up,   blow   up   the trum-pet   in the new moon: ev'n

f   *mf*

lute. Blow   up,   blow   up   the trum-pet   in the new moon: ev'n

f

lute. Blow_____ up,   blow   up   the trum-pet   in the new moon:

f   *mf*

20

in the time ap-point - ed,   and up-on our   so-lemn   feast-

in   the time   ap-point-ed, ev'n in   the   time   ap - point - ed,

in   the time   ap - point - ed,   ap - point - ed, and up-on our

mf

ev'n in   the time ap - point - ed, and up-on our

31. Panis angelicus
(*Bread of the angel host*)

St Thomas Aquinas
(1225–74)
English text by John Rutter

César Franck (1822–90)
arr. John Rutter (b. 1945)

* Transcribed from the original accompaniment for cello, harp, and organ.

This piece (OCCO17) is available separately (ISBN 0–19–341791–X).

pau - per,   pau - per,   ser - vus, et hu - mi - lis.
hum - ble,   low - ly,   all share his sa - cred feast.

Pa - nis an - ge - li - cus   fit   pa - nis
Bread   of the   an - gel host   sent   down from

Pa - nis an - ge - li - cus   fit   pa - nis   ho - mi - num;
Bread   of the   an - gel host   sent   down from   God a - bove;

32. Psalm 150

John Harper
(b. 1947)

The division of forces is optional and may be ignored or altered.

The right hand of the accompaniment may be altered to follow the voice part if need be.

On an organ with 3 manuals, set I (Gt.) to a bright chorus (e.g. 8.4.2), II (Sw.) to a softer chorus with mixture, and III to a solo reed or suitably exciting combination. I & II should not be coupled, unless absolutely necessary, until bar 30.

The Grail translation is used by kind permission of Collins Publishers.

33. Rejoice!

('Arrival of the Queen of Sheba' from Handel's *Solomon*)

Malcolm Archer

Chorus parts by Malcolm Archer
(b. 1952)
to accompaniment of G. F. Handel, arr. M.A.

Re - joice,   re - joice,   and

give him thanks,___ and give him_ thanks._

Spread his name through-out the world, through -

- out the world, O spread his_ name through-out_ the_ world.

through - out the world.

-joice,   re-joice,   and give   him   thanks__ and give   him__ thanks.__

Spread his name through - out the world, the

Spread his name through - out the world, the

Lord is great and to be feared,

Lord is great and to be feared, the

34. Rejoice in the Lord alway

Philippians 4: 4–7

Anon. (mid-16th century, English)
ed. Peter Le Huray
and David Willcocks *

* Additional editorial suggestions are by The Editors. They are given here in square brackets.

35. Rise up, my love, my fair one

Song of Songs 2: 10–12

Healey Willan
(1880–1968)

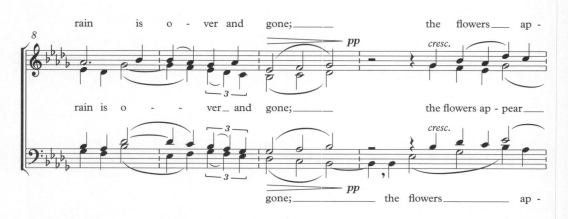

dedicated to the Honourable Ivor Guest and the Lady Mabel Fox-Strangways on the occasion of their marriage. Nov. 22nd 1938.

36. Set me as a seal upon thine heart

adapted from the Song of Songs 8: 6–7

William Walton
(1902–83)

This piece (A86) is available separately (ISBN 0–19–359439–0).

*this piece was written for the wedding of Mark Wilde and
Imogen Wright and was first performed by the choir of St George's Chapel, Windsor,
directed by Jonathan Rees-Williams, on 1st June 1996*

37. Song

Paul Eluard
(1895–1952)
from *Marine*
tr. Gilbert Bowen

Gabriel Jackson
(b. 1962)

Baron's Court
23 April–2 May 1996

commissioned by The Episcopal Church of the Transfiguration, Dallas, Texas,
on the occasion of the 30th anniversary of Howard E. Ross
as Director of Music Ministries and Organist

38. The Invitation

George Herbert
(1593–1632)

Joel Martinson
(b. 1960)

* **I: Principals 8', 4', Flute 8', II/I**
   II: Flutes 8', 4', 2'
   Ped: Principal 16', Flutes 16', 8', I/Ped., II/Ped.

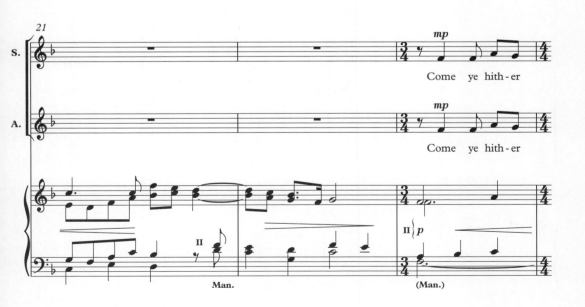

* Original text reads 'daintes', meaning desserts or sweet things. This has been replaced with 'good things' by composer.

bounds: Here   is   joy___   that   drown - eth quite   your de -

bounds: Here   is   joy   that   drown - eth quite   your de -

- light,   as   a flood the low   -   er grounds.

- light,   as   a flood the low   -   er grounds.

poco accel.

rall.

in memoriam Edward T. Chapman

39. The Lord bless you and keep you

Numbers 6: 24

John Rutter
(b. 1945)

This piece (E154) is available separately (ISBN 0–19–351128–2).

A scoring for strings is available on hire.

40. Though I speak with the tongues of men

Edward C. Bairstow
(1874–1946)

1 Corinthians 13: 1–4, 7–9, 12 & 13

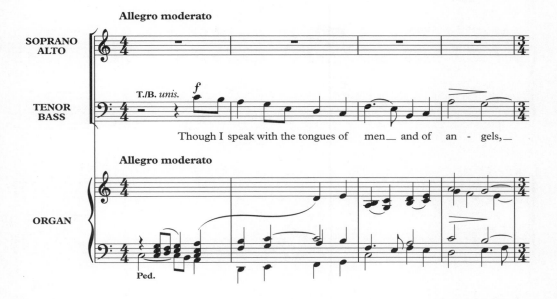

This piece (A63) is available separately (ISBN 0–19–350135–X).

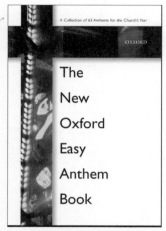